Samuel French Acting Edition

Look Me In The Eye

by Mark L. Massaglia

Copyright © 2003, 2004 by Mark L. Massaglia
All Rights Reserved

LOOK ME IN THE EYE is fully protected under the copyright laws of the United States of America, the British Commonwealth, including Canada, and all other countries of the Copyright Union. All rights, including professional and amateur stage productions, recitation, lecturing, public reading, motion picture, radio broadcasting, television and the rights of translation into foreign languages are strictly reserved.

ISBN 978-0-874-40199-8

www.SamuelFrench.com
www.SamuelFrench.co.uk

FOR PRODUCTION ENQUIRIES

UNITED STATES AND CANADA
Info@SamuelFrench.com
1-866-598-8449

UNITED KINGDOM AND EUROPE
Plays@SamuelFrench.co.uk
020-7255-4302

Each title is subject to availability from Samuel French, depending upon country of performance. Please be aware that *LOOK ME IN THE EYE* may not be licensed by Samuel French in your territory. Professional and amateur producers should contact the nearest Samuel French office or licensing partner to verify availability.

CAUTION: Professional and amateur producers are hereby warned that *LOOK ME IN THE EYE* is subject to a licensing fee. Publication of this play(s) does not imply availability for performance. Both amateurs and professionals considering a production are strongly advised to apply to Samuel French before starting rehearsals, advertising, or booking a theatre. A licensing fee must be paid whether the title(s) is presented for charity or gain and whether or not admission is charged. Professional/Stock licensing fees are quoted upon application to Samuel French.

No one shall make any changes in this title(s) for the purpose of production. No part of this book may be reproduced, stored in a retrieval system, or transmitted in any form, by any means, now known or yet to be invented, including mechanical, electronic, photocopying, recording, videotaping, or otherwise, without the prior written permission of the publisher. No one shall upload this title(s), or part of this title(s), to any social media websites.

For all enquiries regarding motion picture, television, and other media rights, please contact Samuel French.

Please refer to page 30 for further copyright information.

CAST

ANGELA — Middle school student; nonverbal; she uses a wheelchair.

BRUCE — Middle school student; nonverbal; he uses a wheelchair.

KATIE — Middle school student; nonverbal; she uses a wheelchair.

MAX — Middle school student.

CHERISE — Middle school student.

STEPHANIE — Middle school student.

ANGELA'S ADULT — Cares for Angela.

BRUCE'S ADULT — Cares for Bruce.

KATIE'S ADULT — Cares for Katie.

ANGELA'S WHEELER — Faceless person; cares and gestures for Angela.

BRUCE'S WHEELER — Faceless person; cares and gestures for Bruce.

KATIE'S WHEELER — Faceless person; cares and gestures for Katie.

ANGELA'S VOICE — Actor offstage; verbalizes Angela's thoughts.

BRUCE'S VOICE — Actor offstage; verbalizes Bruce's thoughts.

KATIE'S VOICE — Actor offstage; verbalizes Katie's thoughts.

AUTHOR'S NOTES

This play was written based on the lives and backgrounds of specific people. Concerning the students with disabilities in the play, you may or may not have kids who exactly match Angela, Bruce and Katie. It may be necessary for you to alter the script so that it reflects the students with disabilities that you intend to cast or represent in those roles. The play is designed to include three students with disabilities. The playwright would not condone using a student who is not disabled in those roles if it could possibly be avoided, unless in the case of a representational cast.

The students about whom the play is written come from an area of the country that is not culturally diverse. It would be appropriate to change the names of the characters to match those students whom you intend to use in the production. In general, making slight changes in the script to personalize the characters is encouraged.

COSTUMES

Adults – informal clothing.

Wheelers – In black clothing and hoods, white gloves with black on top, and a white mask.. A black backdrop should be used to emphasize their masks and hands. The black side of the gloves are used for gestures around the face, while the white palms are used for gestures away from the face.

Angela – school clothes.

Katie – school clothes.

Bruce – school clothes with a K.C. Chiefs sweatshirt or T-shirt.

Max – school clothes.

Cherise – school clothes.

Stephanie – school clothes.

WHEELERS

The Wheelers serve two main purposes: to attend to their counterparts' needs; to gesture for them during their lines. Needs must take precedence over gesturing. Every movement must be exaggerated. Wheelers should demonstrate the emotion of the lines that are being delivered by their counterparts without upstaging them.

The goal is to have the audience pay attention to Angela, Bruce and Katie. The closer in proximity to their faces the gestures may be performed, the better.

SET

Bare stage with two benches and a stump.

VOICES

Actors performing the voices are offstage should be able to see the actors on stage to allow for any necessary adjustments during the performance. In the premier production the robot-like voices were pre-recorded and given a synthesized quality unless otherwise indicated as a normal-sounding voice.

LOOK ME IN THE EYE

SCENE I

(AT RISE: ANGELA and her ADULT and WHEELER are on and around a bench SL. KATIE and her counterparts are on and around the stump CS. BRUCE and his counterparts are on and around the bench to the right of ANGELA'S ADULTS. WHEELERS are seated with their backs to the audience.)

BRUCE'S ADULT. *(To BRUCE.)* What a beautiful day! Aren't you glad we came to the park?
ANGELA'S ADULT. *(Overlapping. Fussing over Angela. [If ANGELA is smiling or seems tense, comment on that. Make it positive and as though talking to a very small child, making sure she is comfortable.])*
KATIE'S ADULT. *(Overlapping. Fussing likewise over Katie.)*

(ADULTS sit on the benches near their counterparts and act as though They are watching the activities of the park.)

BRUCE'S ADULT. *(Pointing.)* Oh, look! There's a kite! Look Bruce, see how high it is? Wow!
KATIE'S ADULT. Look Katie, at that unusual cloud. . . *(Studies cloud closely.)* It looks like a castle. See, there's the drawbridge and those little clouds around it look

like soldiers standing guard! *(Stares at it for a short while with a dreamy look.)*

ANGELA'S ADULT. *(Immediately.)* Gee, that dog can really jump! He must have jumped eight feet up to get that ball stuck in a tree. Wait a minute! *(Peers closely.)* That's not a ball. It's. . .It's. . .IT'S A SQUIRREL! *(Covering Angela's eyes.)* Don't look, sweetheart, don't look!!!

(CHERISE and STEPHANIE rush onstage in a panic.)

CHERISE. Something terrible has happened! Mrs. Brown told me to get you. She needs your help badly!
KATIE'S ADULT. We can't just leave these kids here by themselves!
CHERISE. I can stay with them and Stephanie can take you to Mrs. Brown.

(Each ADULT briefly attends to their child and then rushes off after STEPHANIE. As the ADULTS leave, each WHEELER stands up like a flower growing in fast motion. They stretch their arms above them until they are completely up and move beside their counterpart. CHERISE looks at all three kids nervously, unsure of what to do.)

CHERISE. *(Nervously, not looking directly at any of the kids.)* H-How are you guys doing? Are you having a good day?
ANGELA. *(ANGELA'S WHEELER helps her activate the switch which appears to operate a voice synthesizer which sounds very robotic whenever she has dialogue.)* How are you?

CHERISE. What? Did one of you speak to me?
ANGELA. How are you?
CHERISE. *(Moving toward ANGELA.)* Oh, it's you!
BRUCE. *(BRUCE'S WHEELER assists with his synthesizer switch likewise.)* How are you?
CHERISE. *(Moving toward BRUCE.)* And you!
KATIE. *(KATIE'S WHEELER performs same switch function as others.)* How are you?
CHERISE. *(Going up to KATIE, and finding the switch, turns toward the audience holding it in full view.)* Oh, I see! You have this switch and a machine which helps you talk. Isn't that wonderful!
ANGELA. May I have a drink of water.

(CHERISE returns KATIE'S switch and moves to ANGELA.)

ANGELA. There is a water bottle attached to my chair.
CHERISE. My goodness! The technology they have created to help you speak is impressive. *(SHE gets the bottle and helps ANGELA take a drink with the help of ANGELA'S WHEELER.)*
ANGELA. Thank you!
CHERISE. You're welcome!
ANGELA. Please sit down and talk with me!
CHERISE. *(Not quite understanding how this is going to work.)* Oh, okay, sure! *(SHE begins to speak to ANGELA too loudly as though she were hard of hearing and a small child.)* Isn't it fun to come to the park, Angela? Look at all the pretty flowers and the birdies!

(ANGELA'S WHEELER begins to activate the switch, but instead turns to ANGELA and then the audience. She then makes a gesture as if asking permission to speak without the switch. This gesture is accompanied by the sound of brushed chimes.)

ANGELA. *(HER voice sounds normal.)* You know it IS fun to come to the park and the flowers and birds ARE pretty, but you don't need to talk to me like I'm some sort of idiot or a child. I AM a teenager for God's sake!

CHERISE. *(Looking at ANGELA with amazement and surprise.)* I... I... I'm sorry. I didn't know whether or not you could understand me.

ANGELA. *(Irritated.)* So you just assumed I could not! Is that it?

CHERISE. I guess you're right. But I meant no offense!

ANGELA. No, I suppose you didn't. I'm sorry to jump all over you, but I'm very sensitive about this. You have no idea how many people treat me like I'm an idiot!

CHERISE. Really! That must get old. I guess most people are like me. They just don't' know.

ANGELA. I guess I shouldn't complain. Most people don't treat me like anything at all. They pretty much ignore me if they can. *(With budding anger.)* I get left out of lots of fun stuff.... AND IT PISSES ME OFF! *(Shocked laughter.)* Oh, my God, I can't believe I said that.

CHERISE. *(Chuckling.)* That's okay, I've heard it before, believe me!

ANGELA. Hey! We don't even know each other's name yet! My name is Angela, what's yours?

CHERISE. Cherise.

ANGELA. Cherise...That's a pretty name. Tell me about yourself, Cherise.

CHERISE. I don't really know what to tell you. What do you want to know?

ANGELA. Just tell me what your life is like. Tell me what you like and don't like. Tell me what you do for fun!

CHERISE. Well, let's see, my mother runs a dance studio so I dance. I also like to swim and listen to music. I like going to school for the most part, especially my Drama class. I like doing well in school and I've got a great family.

ANGELA. That's amazing, Cherise!

CHERISE. What is so amazing about that?

ANGELA. It's amazing because almost everything you said is the same for me. I like to dance and listen to music. I like going to school, especially my Drama class, and I've got a great family. Isn't it wild that we have so much in common? I'll bet you're surprised by that, aren't you?

CHERISE. I guess I am, a little. But as I think about it, I don't really know why! *(Pointing.)* Hey, Angela, look over there. It's Michael Erwin. He's the hottest guy in school, I think. Oh my God, he's walking this way. *(Looks nonchalant while watching him pass.)* Did you see the way he was looking me over?

ANGELA. Oh, he was soooo NOT looking at you. He was looking at ME! And I looked him over pretty good, too. You're right, he IS hot!

CHERISE. *(Teasing.)* Don't you have a boyfriend, Angela? *(Pointing to BRUCE.)* I'll bet you like that guy back there, don't you?

ANGELA. You know, Bruce is a really nice guy, and I do like him, but not as a boyfriend. He and I don't have that much in common. Did you think that I was limited to liking boys with a disability, Cherise?

CHERISE. I guess I really didn't think at all, now that you mention it!

ANGELA. Actually, now that you showed me Michael, I think I may pursue HIM. *(Cherise shakes her head.)* A girl can dream, can't she?

CHERISE. Do you, Angela?

ANGELA. Do I what?

CHERISE. Do you dream? Do you dream about what might have been?

ANGELA. Oh, yes! I dream all the time. But not about what might have been. I dream about what will be!

CHERISE. What do you mean?

ANGELA. You are like most people. They expect me to have dreams and goals based on my disability. They think that I'm hoping that some day some miracle will happen and I'll be able to win the Olympic gymnastics competition. But my goals and dreams relate to who I really am! You know? I dream of actually having a real, meaningful, fulfilling career. A job that will make me happy. A job that will give me the chance to make others happy! My biggest dream is for people to see beyond my disability. To see ME for who I am, right here, right now! A kid in school... a loyal friend... a happy person... a girl who likes a boy like Michael to say "Hi" to me in the hall... a girl who wants to be popular as much as everyone else. I dream of the day when people will think of me as just plain old Angela instead of the Poor Little Disabled Girl. That's not too much to ask, is it Cherise?

CHERISE. No, it sure isn't!

ANGELA. Then you'll sort of understand why I get mad sometimes when people won't look at me for who I am!

CHERISE. Believe me, I DO understand. I didn't until you explained it. I wish everyone could hear your side of the story. Maybe they'd behave differently.

ANGELA. Now that YOU understand, other people CAN hear my side of the story! .....Cherise?

CHERISE. Yes, Angela?

ANGELA. Do you ever get mad about things?

CHERISE. *(Laughing.)* Oh, if you were around me more you'd know that I get mad often! Actually I have a reputation for being. . . sort of crabby!

ANGELA. What kinds of things make you mad?

CHERISE. *(Pausing and looking thoughtful.)* Lot's of things. . . getting a bad grade, bombing a test, not understanding my homework. . . people calling me dumb. All of those things make me angry. I HATE being teased. . . especially by guys, or by anyone for that matter. . . I hate getting up early. . . I get mad when my hair won't cooperate when I'm trying to get ready for school. . . I get angry when I can't get something I'm trying to learn. That's especially true of dancing. *(Stands and continues.)* My mom is extra hard on me in dance class. I guess she feels like if I am not catching on it makes her look like failure. She's constantly getting on me for every little mistake I make, especially when we are learning some new choreography. The other day she was trying to teach us this new dance routine and I just couldn't get it! I mean, I'm a good dancer and usually I pick thing up pretty fast. . . but for some reason. . . this one step. . . *(With growing frustration.)* . . .I just couldn't get it, and she was embarrassed. The more embarrassed she got the harder I tried, and the harder I tried the worse I got! By the end of the session I was so mad I was crying and so was my mom! Well, you get the picture.

ANGELA.. Cherise, I want to stand up and I need your help.

CHERISE. What should I do?

ANGELA. Will you hand onto my arms?

(CHERISE and ANGELA'S WHEELER help ANGELA stand up. ANGELA takes a few steps with CHERISE holding her hands, CHERISE looking her in the eye the whole time.)

ANGELA. You know what, Cherise? It makes me very happy when I get a chance to get out of that chair and walk. Very happy! I just wish I didn't get tired as easily so I could do it more often. Can you help me back to my chair? *(CHERISE and the WHEELER help ANGELA get back in her chair.)* Thank you. You'll get your dance step someday, Cherise. Don't focus on what you can NOT do, be happy about what you CAN do!

CHERISE. *(CHERISE hugs ANGELA.)* Thank you!

(STEPHANIE enters from SL.)

STEPHANIE. Hi, Cherise! How have things been going? What have you been doing?

CHERISE. *(Still near ANGELA and looking her directly in the eye.)* I've been having a heart-to-heart talk with my new friend, Angela!

STEPHANIE. Mrs. Brown wants you to bring Angela to her. She told me to stay here with the other kids.

CHERISE. Okay, I'll be glad to do that. Come on Angela, let's go!
ANGELA. *(ANGELA'S WHEELER helps her push the switch and her voice is synthesized again.)* Angela will go with you. *(CHERISE looks a little surprised.)*
STEPHANIE. Wow! That is amazing technology, isn't it?

(CHERISE kneels down and looks at ANGELA.)

CHERISE. It's even more amazing than you realize, but not nearly as amazing as this girl! Let's go, Angela. *(ANGELA and CHERISE exit SL. ANGELA'S WHEELER follows CHERISE with one hand on CHERISE's shoulder. Stephanie waves.)*

SCENE II

(STEPHANIE looks around nervously, unsure of what to do. Moves CS.)

STEPHANIE. *(Nervously, not looking directly at any of the kids.)* H-How are you guys doing? Are you having a good day in the park?
KATIE. *(KATIE'S WHEELER helps her press her synthesizer switch.)* How are you?
STEPHANIE. What?! Did one of you speak to me?
KATIE. How are you?
STEPHANIE. *(Moving toward KATIE.)* Oh, it's you!

BRUCE. How are you?

STEPHANIE. *(Turning to BRUCE.)* And you! *(Picking up BRUCE'S switch for the audience to see.)* Oh, I see! You have this switch to the machine which helps you talk. Isn't that wonderful?!

KATIE. Will you please wipe my chin for me?

(STEPHANIE returns BRUCE'S switch to him and moves to KATIE, nervous at having to attend to one of the kids.)

STEPHANIE. Wipe your chin? Well, of course, but how should I do that? *(SHE looks around for water.)*

KATIE. There is a towel on my lap.

STEPHANIE. My goodness! The things they have created to help you speak are impressive. *(SHE gets the bottle and helps KATIE take a drink with the assistance of KATIE'S WHEELER.)*

KATIE. Thank you.

STEPHANIE. *(Speaking as if KATIE were deaf.)* YOU'RE WELCOME!

KATIE. My name is Katie, what is yours?

STEPHANIE. *(Loudly.)* MY NAME IS STEPHANIE. I'M SORRY THAT I DIDN'T ALREADY KNOW YOUR NAME. I GUESS WE DON'T SEE EACH OTHER VERY OFTEN.

KATIE. I see you almost every day.

STEPHANIE. Oh! *(To herself.)* No, that can't be right. . . can it?

(KATIE'S WHEELER begins to activate the switch, then turns instead to KATIE, then toward the AUDIENCE. She then makes a gesture as

if to ask permission to speak without the switch. This gesture is accompanied by the sound of brushed chimes.)

KATIE.   I guess it's easy not to notice me down here! Please sit down and talk with me.

STEPHANIE.   *(Still loudly and as if to a small child.)* Oh, okay, but if you don't mind I think I'll stand. I've been sitting all day. If I sit too long it drives me crazy.

(KATIE'S WHEELER comes around to KATIE's side and assumes a position of scorn and disbelief. Pointing out to STEPHANIE the obvious; that KATIE sits in a chair all day, every day.)

STEPHANIE.   Oh my God! That was an insensitive thing to say, wasn't it? *(SHE leans down to say loudly to KATIE.)*   I'M SORRY! I DIDN'T MEAN TO BE INSENSITIVE!!

KATIE.   You know, I don't now which is worse— you being insensitive, or talking to me like I'm a hearing-impaired BABY!

STEPHANIE.   *(Chagrined.)*   See there, I did it again! I really should think about what I say*!*

KATIE.   I won't hold it against you for being insensitive, if you don't hold it against ME for calling you AN IDIOT! *(Embarrassed.)* Gosh, I can't believe I said that. I don't know what came over me. Sometimes I just get so mad. You know what I mean?

STEPHANIE.   Yes, I do. I have a lot of things that make me mad!

KATIE.   Like what?

STEPHANIE. *(Sitting on the stump.)* Oh gee, let's see... where should I start? One thing that really bothers me is when other people are talking or making noise when I am trying to concentrate. I just can't study when there's a lot of noise.

KATIE. Really? I sort of like a little noise. I think it's great when people are busy doing things.

STEPHANIE. It also bothers me when I don't do well on my school work, or I don't have time to get my homework done because of the sports I play, or because the teacher assigned too much! I hate it when I don't do well in basketball practice, too! I hate it when I get teased and I hate it when I see other people get teased.

KATIE. Sometimes it hurts just as bad when someone makes an insensitive remark as it does when someone teases.

STEPHANIE. Oh, yeah! I forgot to say that I hate it when someone keeps reminding me about insensitive remarks I made a L-O-N-G time ago!

KATIE. Okay! Fair enough. I'll try not to be insensitive about your having made insensitive remarks!

STEPHANIE. *(Chuckling.)* Oh, brother! Hey, Katie, what about you? Are there things that bug you other than... you know?

KATIE. Of course! I'm no different than anyone else. There are things that happen that bug me. A lot of the same things that bother you, as a matter of fact! I guess the difference is that it probably takes a lot less to make me happy than you and your friends. I like to think I enjoy and appreciate the simple things in life.

STEPHANIE. Oh, yeah? Like what for instance?

KATIE. I love to go for walk and drives. I like to swim, and I love it when school gets cancelled because of snow.

STEPHANIE. Me, too! That's a good one.

KATIE. I love to hear people singing, and I love to have people talking to me like you are right now. Did you ever hear that song by John Denver about Sunshine? I think one of the things I enjoy most is to go outside and feel the sunshine on my face. That really makes me happy!

STEPHANIE. I envy you, Katie. I've gotten all wrapped up in having to have things that cost money, to be happy. Or, at least I think I have. I guess I've outgrown the kind of things you're talking about . It seems now when I think of things that make me happy, they are either at the mall or depend on me doing well in sports.

KATIE. It doesn't have to be that way! We all have the same basic needs, and if we have some food, a roof over our heads and some clothes to wear, we ought to consider ourselves pretty lucky because a lot of kids don't. Come on Steph! Take a walk on the wild side. . . Next time your friends ask you if you want to go shopping, you just tell them you'd rather go over to Katie's house, sit on the porch, and feel the sunshine on your face. *(Laughing.)* Man, I'd love to see the expressions on their faces!

STEPHANIE. *(Defensively.)* You never know, I might just do that someday! *(Beat.)* Katie? You seem so positive about things. Don't you ever get down about having to use a wheelchair all the time? Don't you wish you didn't have to use it so you could be in sports and be more active?

KATIE. I do wish I didn't have to sit in this chair all the time, and it bothers me that I can't tall people what I want or how I feel. I'm not able to talk to other people like I am to you. But even though sometimes I do get irritated about having a disability, I think I should work it into my life rather than to work my life around the disability. I can be in sports. I swim, I go to intramurals, I go on field trips. I do many of the things that kids without disabilities do. Why not be thankful for being able to do the things I CAN, rather than being hung up about the things I CAN'T?

STEPHANIE.   Wow. . .You're right, of course. But I don't think my attitude would be as good as yours if I were in your shoes.

KATIE.   Steph, no offense, but your attitude isn't as good as mine is, right now! You really ought to work on being more positive.

STEPHANIE.   *(Laughing.)*   Now look who's being insensitive! *(Beat.)* Katie? What about boys? Do you ever think about boys? What about Bruce over there? Is he your boyfriend?

KATIE.   PUH–LEEEZE!! Bruce??? You've got to be kidding! The boy is a country music freak! He'd play it twenty-four hours a day if they'd let him. I HATE country music! Besides, now I have my sights on a new guy. . . Michael Erwin. That cute one with the cute bod. I saw him earlier and he's HOT!

CHERISE   *(Offstage. Calling loudly.)*   Stephanie! Hang in there, we're sending Max over to stay with Bruce while you bring Katie back, okay?

STEPHANIE.   *(Turning from KATIE toward SL. Calling loudly back.)*   Okay! No hurry, everything is fine! *(Turning back toward KATIE and speaking with a sense of urgency.)* Katie, they'll be here in a minute, and we may not get a chance to talk like this again. Is there anything I can do for you? Anything at all? Tell me now!

KATIE.   Yes! Since you ask, there are several things that you can do for me.

STEPHANIE. Anything! Just name it.

KATIE. The first thing you can do for me is to be a more positive person. Steph, be happy about all the good things in your life. Don't get hung up with negative things, okay?

STEPHANIE. Okay, I promise. What else?

KATIE. The second thing you can do for me is to look down once in a while!

STEPHANIE. What do you mean?

KATIE. HELLO! Remember? We live on the same block and go to the same school, and you didn't even know who I was? Look down once in a while so you'll see me. Now that we're friends, I don't want to lose you even if we won't be able to talk like this again. Okay?

STEPHANIE. You didn't have to ask me for that! I won't forget you now. Is there anything else?

KATIE. When I was telling you about all the things I enjoy I life, I forgot to tell you one of the most important. . .

STEPHANIE. What is it? *(She leans close in to KATIE.)*

KATIE. *(Beat.)* Hugs. I love to get hugs!

(STEPHANIE leans down and embraces KATIE.)

STEPHANIE. Oh Katie, I'm so glad I met you! Thank you for sharing with me, it meant a lot!

KATIE. *(Activating her switch with the help of her WHEELER.)* You are welcome.

(Enter MAX from SL.)

MAX. Hi, Stephanie! How's it going? Mrs. Brown sent me to tell you to bring Katie to her. I'll stay here with Bruce.

STEPHANIE. Okay, no problem!

MAX. What have you been doing all this time?

STEPHANIE. I've had a wonderful time. . . just sitting here feeling the worm sunshine on my face! I can't remember when I've enjoyed a day in the park quite as much!

(KATIE and STEPHANIE exit SL. KATIE'S WHEELER follows STEPHANIE with one hand on her shoulder. MAX waves goodbye.)

SCENE III

(MAX is clearly uncomfortable, unable to look directly at BRUCE or be physically near him.)

MAX. *(To BRUCE.)* Hi. Umm, how's it going?

BRUCE. *(BRUCE'S WHEELER helps him activate his synthesizer swtich.)* I am fine, thank you.

MAX. That's amazing! I didn't know there was a machine that could allow you to talk to people. *(From a distance MAX strains to see the device and switch.)* My name is Max. Mrs. Brown asked me if I'd come and stay with you for a while.

BRUCE. My name is Bruce. I am glad you are here.

MAX. It... It's no problem. But I really don't know what I should do. Is there something that I could do for you?

BRUCE. You already have.

MAX. What? What do you mean?

(BRUCE'S WHEELER begins to activate the switch, then turns to BRUCE and then the audience. He then makes a gesture as if to ask permission to speak without the switch. This gesture is accompanied by the sound of brushed chimes.)

BRUCE. *(With a distinct Southern "country" accent.)* You already have done something. Y'all got them gabby gals outta here. Lordie! I thought they was gonna talk me into my grave! Ya see, when a bunch of gals *(With sarcasm—WHEELER makes quote signs with hands.)* "get in touch with their feelings" you just never know what's gonna happen! I ain't used to Katie and Angela sayin' much, anyhow! Now that I've heard how MUCH they say when they can talk, well, I ain't sure that it's all that much of an improvement! Know what I mean?

MAX. I see. But now it's just us guys sort of hanging out together. Hey, the girls DO have their place, right?

BRUCE. You betcha they do! Whoooee!

MAX. You got a girlfriend, Bruce? What about Angela and Katie? Either one of them your gal?

BRUCE. Let me tell ya somethin', just between us guys... *(WHEELER gestures for MAX to come closer, and does so, but still not too close.)* ...they BOTH want me BAD! They're CRAZY 'bout me—but it ain't gonna happen. Don't get me wrong, they're both nice girls, and I like 'em both as friends, but they ain't my type. Katie don't like country music, so that puts the kibosh on her—and Angela...well, she's jes' too sophisticated fer my likin'! As a matter of fact, I kinda got my eye on that Cherise gal that was a-talkin' to Angela earlier. I gotta pick the right time to make my move though!

MAX. I don't want to be...I don't know...mean, or anything....

BRUCE. You kin' talk straight with me MAX! You don't need to pull no punches.

MAX. Your disability? Doesn't that kind of get in the way with girls?

BRUCE. You're sure right about that Max! Ya see, I got what they call Tubular Sclerosis. Along with keepin' me in this chair most of the time, it causes me to drool. Did ya ever try and make a move on some gal with slobber runnin' down your chin?

MAX. Can't say as I have.

BRUCE. Well, I'll tell ya Max... it don't help things much. But the chair, see, that has sorta been good. Gals is always fightin' to see who can push me in my chair!

MAX. Are there other things about being disabled that bug you, Bruce?

BRUCE. One of my teachers asked our class to finish the sentence, "My life is like...". I thought about it, and basically my life is a lot like yours. I get up early for school, I have breakfast and get on the bus. I go to school – sometimes I like it, sometimes I don't. I like hangin' back with my friends, relaxin' watchin' a rodeo or a ball game, or listening to Randy Travis or Garth, and eatin' some Tex-Mex food.

MAX. *(With his back to BRUCE.)* We have a lot in common! Don't we? I didn't realize that until now.

BRUCE. Ya see, Max! That gets to one of the things that really puts a burr under my saddle. I hate it when I get left out of things. It makes me feel bad wen other kids won't include me, won't talk to me, go out of their way to avoid me.

MAX. They're like me Bruce. They just don't know! I don't know how to relate to you, I'll admit it. I feel– *(Hesitates, embarrassed to say what he's thinking.)* ...un ... uncomfortable around people like you.

BRUCE. *(Cynically, with increasing anger. Yelling.)* Oh, I see! Poor Max! He feels uncomfortable around people like me!! DO YOU PITY US, MAX? DOES IT BOTHER YOU TO LOOK AT US?? HEY EVERYBODY, WE MAKE MAX FEEL UNEASY!!!

MAX. *(Taken aback by BRUCE's anger.)* Hey, wait a minute!

BRUCE. Gee, Max, I'm sorry that my disability causes you such terrible problems. . .I FEEL PLUM AWFUL THAT I INTRUDE ON YOUR HAPPINESS!

MAX. Hey, you got it all wrong!

BRUCE. WANT ME TO GO LOCK MYSELF UP SO YOU DON'T HAVE TO SEE ME?

MAX. *(Pleading.)* Bruce, please!

BRUCE. WOULD THAT MAKE IT EASIER FOR YOU???

MAX. BRUCE, STOP IT, PLEASE! I'm begging ya! Why are you talking to me like this? That's not what I meant. Please. . . stop it! You're making me feel bad.

BRUCE. *(Pauses and lowers his tone and responds compassionately.)* It's no fun to be made to feel bad, is it Max?

Now you got a little taste of what we feel like when we're rejected. . . and left out. . . and not included.

MAX. *(Pleading for forgiveness.)* I'm sorry, Bruce. I don't know what to do. I needed to talk with you or someone like you before now, but that wasn't possible. What do I have to do to make it right?

BRUCE. YOU GOTTA LOOK ME IN THE EYE, MAX! You have to look over here, and see more than a wheelchair with somethin' in it! You gotta look me in the eye to know I'm a person, just like you—a person with the same sort of wants, and needs, and likes, and dislikes, and dreams, and goals as YOU. You gotta look – me – in – the – eye. Can ya do it, MAX?

MAX. *(MAX slowly turns around and moves toward BRUCE.)* Yes, Bruce, I can do that. I CAN look you in the eye. *(MAX kneels down beside BRUCE and looks him right in the eyes.)* I see you, Bruce. I see that it IS YOU.

BRUCE. *(Beat.)* I'm a good lookin' feller, ain't I, Max?

MAX. *(Laughing.)* Yes, Bruce, you are! *(*Beat.)* Bruce, are there other things that bother you about having a disability?

BRUCE. Oh, I guess so. I'm sleepy all the time, so I miss out on a lot of stuff. Heck, the other day, I slept completely through a rock concert that we had at school. 'Course I don't mind that much, 'cause I don't care for rock music. Somebody told me that one of 'em sung that "Chattahoochie" song by Alan Jackson, and I love that song! I also regret that normally I can't talk to people the way I'm talking to you. But, I can almost always make people understand how I'm feeling.

MAX. I see by your sweatshirt that you're a Chiefs fan. That's cool. They're my favorite team, too.

BRUCE. That reminds me of another thing that bothers me about my disability. I'm unable to dress by myself. Between that and not being able to talk to folks, I ain't been able to get anyone to understand that I HATE THE STINKIN' CHIEFS! They always got me in a Chiefs shirt or something with the Chiefs on it. It drives me CRAZY!

MAX. Well, if you don't like the Chiefs, who do you like?

BRUCE. Well, like any self-respecting country boy, I root for the Cowboys!

CHERISE. *(Calling from offstage.)* Max! Mrs. Brown said to tell you that someone will be there to pick up Bruce in a minute.

MAX. *(Calling back.)* No problem! We're ready any time!

BRUCE. Well, pardner, it looks like this may be the end of the trail. They'll be here in a minute.

MAX. Why does that mean that anything has to end? As far as I'm concerned, this is just the beginning. Now that I've had a chance to get to know you, I'm not just gonna walk away. You've taught me some valuable stuff today, Bruce, and I thank you for it.

BRUCE. *(Activating synthesizer switch.)* Thank you, Max.

(BRUCE'S ADULT enters with CHERISE and STEPHANIE.)

BRUCE'S ADULT. Ready to go, Bruce? Let's get you back. . .

MAX. Wait! *(HE runs over to BRUCE, looks him right in the eye.)* Goodbye, Bruce. See you around. . . Pardner.

(BRUCE'S ADULT proceeds to help BRUCE offstage. BRUCE'S WHEELER follows behind BRUCE'S ADULT with hand on her shoulder. MAX, CHERISE and STEPHANIE wave from SL and then move CS.)

CHERISE. Wow! It looks like you and Bruce hit it off.

MAX. Yes, we did! He's a very cool guy. I learned a lot from him.

STEPHANIE. You know the same thing happened to me when I spent time with Katie!

CHERISE. Angela and I really hit it off, too. I can't really describe it, but it's the first time that I've really gotten to know someone like that!

STEPHANIE. Me too! I can't really put my finger on it.

MAX. Bruce explained it to me. For the very first time we really looked someone right in the eye.... and it was amazing! Come on guys, let's go.

(Lights down. Benches and stump are removed. Either from a recording, or live, the actors who played the VOICES rise up to a standing position behind a scrim in shadow box lighting, each actor's lighting brightens to full as they say their line. BRUCE'S VOICE is wearing a cowboy hat, KATIE'S VOICE is costumed similarly to KATIE, ANGELA'S VOICE is wearing a dance outfit.)

ANGELA'S VOICE. Do you see us? *(Pirouettes and stays in a dance position after her line.)*
KATIE'S VOICE. We are here! *(Holds hands toward AUDIENCE, palms upward.)*
BRUCE'S VOICE. We're people—we ain't chairs! *(Tips hat.)*

(Blackout.)

* * *

MUSIC USE NOTE

Licensees are solely responsible for obtaining formal written permission from copyright owners to use copyrighted music in the performance of this play and are strongly cautioned to do so. If no such permission is obtained by the licensee, then the licensee must use only original music that the licensee owns and controls. Licensees are solely responsible and liable for all music clearances and shall indemnify the copyright owners of the play(s) and their licensing agent, Samuel French, against any costs, expenses, losses and liabilities arising from the use of music by licensees. Please contact the appropriate music licensing authority in your territory for the rights to any incidental music.

IMPORTANT BILLING AND CREDIT REQUIREMENTS

If you have obtained performance rights to this title, please refer to your licensing agreement for important billing and credit requirements.

www.ingramcontent.com/pod-product-compliance
Lightning Source LLC
Chambersburg PA
CBHW052000290426
44110CB00015B/2317